I0473840

The Insider's Guide to
Legal Fees:
What You NEED to
Know
Before Hiring an Attorney

Jennifer R. Lewis Kannegieter

ISBN-13: 978-1477504017

ISBN-10: 147750401X

Table of Contents

Introduction 5

1 Types of Legal Fees 7

2. Understanding How Fees are Determined 11

3. Different Approaches to Running a Practice 17

4. Five Lawyers to Watch Out For.................................. 23

5. Don't Try This At Home! 29

6. How to Choose an Attorney 31

7. Seven Tips that Can Save You Thousands 37

8. The Value of A Lawyer 45

Conclusion 55

Appendix A: Questions To Ask Before Hiring 57

Appendix B: Retainer Agreement Checklist 59

Appendix C: Client's File 61

About the Author 63

Introduction

Legal fees can be overwhelming. Everyone has heard horror stories about how expensive lawyers can be. Few attorneys will take the time to explain the potential costs involved in a legal action, and even fewer will offer suggestions regarding what a client may do to save on legal fees.

For many people in need of legal services, the fear of getting hit by a high bill is enough to prevent them from seeking legal advice. Instead, they try to solve their problems themselves and seek out forms or advice on the Internet. Unfortunately, this approach often causes more harm than good.

For those who do choose to hire an attorney, they are often asked to sign a retainer agreement (a contract outlining the scope of the lawyer's services and basis for fees) with terms they don't understand. This can cause increased anxiety over the legal matter and pending legal fees.

As an attorney, I have seen firsthand how misconceptions about lawyers and legal fees get in the way of seeking legal advice. Far too many people think they can navigate the legal system without a lawyer. They fumble their way through, and only once it is too late do they learn just how much this mistake has cost them. And quite honestly, hiring the wrong lawyer can be just as bad as trying to handle the legal system without a lawyer.

The wrong lawyer can mismanage your case, draft sloppy documents, and even charge you unnecessarily high fees. The wrong lawyer can fail to explain the legal process, or even the options that are open to you. Hiring the wrong lawyer can leave you feeling lost. Worse, hiring the wrong lawyer can leave you unable to afford hiring the right lawyer.

Every month I am approached by a new potential client who has made the mistake of either not hiring a lawyer, or hiring the wrong lawyer to handle their initial matter. Sadly, for some of these people there is nothing I can do to fix their situation – it is simply too late. For those I can help, most usually end up paying more in legal fees than they would have had they hired the right lawyer from the start. Through the years I have grown increasingly frustrated and disheartened for these people. If only they had known what to expect when it comes to working with a lawyer and what to expect regarding legal fees *before* they needed a lawyer.

The purpose of this book is to provide an insider's perspective about how legal fees are determined, what factors come into play, and how you can control your legal fees. It is my hope that by reading this book you will have a better understanding of how lawyers charge for their services and that a fear of legal fees will no longer be a barrier to seeking the legal advice you need.

Chapter 1
Types of Legal Fees

The first step in understanding legal fees is to learn about the different types of fees. Your legal bill will include both the fees for legal services as well as costs and expenses associated with your case.

Fees for Legal Services

Lawyers charge for their services in a variety of ways; the most common arrangements are contingent fee, hourly fee, and flat fee.

Contingent fee billing means the attorney will receive a predetermined percentage of the settlement or judgment. The attorney does not get paid unless the case is won. The retainer agreement will determine how costs and expenses are handled – whether the client will pay those upfront, as they are incurred, or if they will initially be paid by the attorney and reimbursed out of the settlement.

This type of fee is most common in personal injury cases or in some civil litigation cases where a monetary award is expected. Contingent billing is prohibited in certain cases, such as divorce and other family law matters.

Hourly billing is the most common arrangement and is the default structure for legal fees. You pay a certain amount per hour for all time the lawyer or the lawyer's office spends on your case. An attorney's hourly rate can vary greatly depending on several factors including location, experience, and the individual attorney. It is common for different people in the same office to charge at different rates – a senior attorney will charge more than a junior attorney; and a paralegal or assistant will charge less than an attorney. An attorney's rate may also depend on the type of activity performed (i.e. a higher rate for time spent in court or a lower rate for travel).

With an hourly billing structure, it is important to understand not only what the rates are, but how time is billed. Most lawyers will charge to the nearest one tenth of an hour (6 minute increments), but some may charge to the nearest quarter of an hour (15 minute increments).

For an hourly fee case, it is common for the client to pay a retainer fee upfront, before work starts on their case. The retainer fee is paid when you hire (or retain) the attorney and is kept in a special trust account (also known as an IOLTA). As your case progresses, the lawyer will send you an invoice, and then pay themselves from the money held in the IOLTA account. The attorney will require the client to replenish the funds held in the trust account if the progression of the case exceeds the amount of the retainer remaining in the trust account.

Flat fee billing is typically used in routine, uncontested matters such as simple estate planning or business formations. The price is set (and typically paid) before the work starts, so you know exactly how much it will cost you. A good flat fee agreement will specify what is, and is not, included and who is responsible for additional out-of-pocket expenses.

While contingent, hourly, and flat fee are the most common arrangements, there has been recent talk in the legal world about "**alternative**" or "**value**" billing. Although there is no concrete definition for these terms, these arrangements are typically a version of a flat fee.

With alternative or value billing a traditionally hourly, contested matter may be broken down into various subsections, each offered for a flat fee. Alternatively, the lawyer may offer services based upon a monthly rate, similar to a subscription plan. A lawyer may also use these terms to market unbundled services. With unbundled, or limited legal services, the lawyer only provides limited representation and is not responsible for the entire case. Before falling for the terms "alternative" or "value," find out exactly what they mean to the lawyer using them.

While there are common approaches to the type of fees used in various areas of law (i.e. personal injury cases are contingent fees and divorce cases are based on an hourly fee), some lawyers offer different types of fees to set themselves apart from their competition; just because most of the lawyers in your city use hourly fees does not mean they all do. When looking for a lawyer, be sure to ask what type of fee arrangement they use for cases like yours.

Costs and Expenses

In addition to the fees you will incur for legal services, there may be out of pocket expenses that you will also be responsible for paying. These expenses may include court filing fees, mediators, evaluators, expert witnesses, and other professionals. In a contested case the costs for court fees and professional services can quickly add up to several thousands of dollars.

Sometimes these expenses are paid for out of the retainer account (or included in the flat fee), but often the client is expected to pay these fees as they are incurred. These fees could be billed through your lawyer's office, or they could be paid directly to the court or the professional. It is a good idea to ask your attorney in advance what fees you can expect and how those fees will be handled.

There may also be additional administrative expenses for your case including fees for photocopies, parking, and phone charges. Some law firms will treat expenses such as copying, postage, and mileage as a cost of doing business and take the expense as a tax deduction; others will pass those costs along to the clients. Some firms may have a policy that expenses over a certain dollar amount are charged to the client, while other firms may pass on all expenses to the client. In these firms each stamp is counted before mailing and each copy is counted as it is produced to be included as an expense on your invoice. While these expenses may not add much to the total invoice, it can be irritating to see the additional cost of stamps and copies in addition to what you are already paying for the lawyer's services. Before hiring a lawyer, make sure you understand how these expenses will be treated.

Chapter 2
How Fees Are Determined

Knowing the different types of legal fees commonly used is just the first step. To fully understand legal fees you need to know how fees are determined and how they are paid.

Setting Fees

The American Bar Association (ABA) Model Rules of Professional Conduct Rule 1.5 prohibits an attorney from "charging or collecting an unreasonable fee or an unreasonable amount for expenses." The rule further provides that the following factors are considered when determining whether or not the fee is reasonable:

(1) the time and labor required, the novelty and difficulty of the questions involved, and the skill requisite to perform the legal service properly;

(2) the likelihood, if apparent to the client, that the acceptance of the particular employment will preclude other employment by the lawyer;

(3) the fee customarily charged in the locality for similar legal services;

(4) the amount involved and the results obtained;

(5) the time limitations imposed by the client or by the circumstances;

(6) the nature and length of the professional relationship with the client;

(7) the experience, reputation, and ability of the lawyer or lawyers performing the services; and

(8) whether the fee is fixed or contingent.

- ABA Model Rules of Professional Conduct Rule 1.5(a)

Most states have their own rules of professional responsibility based upon those of the ABA. However, while the rules aim to provide some guidelines for lawyers and their clients, Rule 1.5 does not provide a clear-cut way of calculating what a reasonable fee should be.

As you can see from Rule 1.5(a), several different factors go into determining whether a fee is reasonable. It is not always easy to know if a fee is reasonable. How exactly do you determine the skill of the lawyer or the difficulty of the question? How do you know what fees are customarily charged?

Additionally, people are often uncomfortable talking about money in a private setting, and anti-trust laws prevent the discussion of fees among lawyers in a formalized setting.

Standard rates will vary greatly depending on several factors including location, experience, and the area of law in which a lawyer practices. This means that the hourly rate for an attorney can be under $200 or over $1,000. An hourly rate could be based upon a lawyer's experience, the lawyer's overhead expenses, or what other lawyers in the area charge. A flat fee or a retainer fee may be calculated based upon the anticipated time or effort involved or the "value" to the client for the work in question. Sometimes there may be no rhyme nor reason to the rate.

Making Payments

Most attorneys will require an upfront payment upon being hired. In many cases, this payment is considered a retainer payment and is generally held in a trust account. This initial fee is usually refundable if not earned. While these safeguards are required by attorney ethical rules, there may be some exceptions or differences depending on the jurisdiction.

Attorney ethical rules can also have different restrictions on credit card payments and trust accounts. Because of these rules, some lawyers are not able to, or are not willing to, accept payments by credit card. If you plan to pay with a credit card, make sure you ask the lawyer if he or she can accept payments that way.

Sometimes paying legal fees may be a hardship. It may be difficult to make one large payment, but making several smaller payments would allow you to afford an attorney. Some attorneys may be willing to work out a payment schedule for you, but only if you ask for, or suggest, a plan.

Pro Bono and Sliding Fee Services

Many people worry they cannot afford a lawyer. As I stated previously, paying a lawyer can be difficult for clients at any economic level. For those clients truly living near the poverty level, there may still be options.

In very limited cases, you may be entitled to a free, court-appointed attorney. Though as courts and governments face a severe budget crisis, programs have been cut and court-appointed attorneys remain available only in those cases required by the state or federal constitutions, such as representing criminal defendants.

There are a variety of legal aid offices and non-profit agencies offering *pro bono* (Latin, meaning "for the public good") services, ranging from self-help clinics to full legal representation. These services are free to those who qualify. However, an application process will be required to assess your financial need. Financial need is typically met if you are receiving, or could qualify for, public assistance or welfare services.

Agencies are generally limited in the type of case or location serviced. Some agencies utilize in-house lawyers to serve their clients, while others rely on volunteers from the local legal community. Most agencies have long waiting lists and must prioritize the type of case. Even if you meet the agencies' requirements, you may not be accepted, or you might need to wait several months, due to overwhelming caseloads. If your case is time-sensitive, or if you are responding to or defending against an action, you will be unable to wait for a pro bono opening. Some agencies may have law clinics where individuals who are unable to get representation can at least get legal advice and limited assistance on their case.

Please be advised that most private attorneys will only accept pro bono cases through an agency. However, some private attorneys are willing to accept cases on a sliding fee basis. If an attorney is willing to do this, an application process is typically required, and the attorney may still require an upfront retainer (but charge a lower rate for legal services). The attorney may also limit the number of sliding fee cases accepted.

Chapter 3
Different Approaches to Running a Practice

A law firm is a business, and just like any other industry there are different ways to manage a business. Incidentally, how a law firm is run can have a direct impact on legal fees, as this will affect the firm's business practices. Answering the following questions will help you to determine the type of firm, and how they may best handle your case.

What is the firm's business attitude?

A business concerned about creating customer goodwill and maintaining a reputation will likely have more reasonable fees than a business trying to make a quick million. Working with a quality business usually means a quality product at a reasonable price. Developing a relationship with a quality business can be mutually beneficial for years to come. Choosing a questionable business can result in sub-par work and unreasonable expenses. Unfortunately, it is not always easy to distinguish quality businesses from questionable ones until it is too late. Law firms are no different.

In choosing a lawyer it is important to consider how that lawyer's firm operates as a business. The way a firm is managed can provide insight on how the lawyer will handle your case.

What is the firm's case load?

Some law firms operate as "mills" - servicing a large number of clients as quickly as possible; other firms maintain smaller caseloads with the goal of providing personalized attention to each client. A law firm with too many clients can rarely provide the same level of customer service and individualized attention that a firm with fewer clients will.

Some law firms limit the types of cases they accept; others accept any type of case that walks in the door. While it may be appealing to use the law firm down the street for all of your legal needs, your needs may be best met by choosing the right lawyer for the particular case. You wouldn't ask your family doctor to delivery your baby, perform brain surgery on your spouse, replace your mother's knee, or handle your father's heart surgery.

What is the firm's overhead?

Some firms are concerned with impressing clients by a fancy office space or expensive advertising; other firms operate on a shoestring budget. A firm with high monthly expenses needs to generate that much more in revenue each month just to keep up. A firm that keeps expenses low; or that allows expenses to adjust based on the current level of business will experience less stress.

What is the firms' use of associates, assistants, and staff?

This is one of the most challenging aspects of a firm's business approach to evaluate. Attorneys who do everything themselves are often wasting their own time on tasks that could be more efficiently completed by someone else, so the use of staff can be a good thing - depending on how the staff is used and the communication that occurs within the firm.

Some firms will use associates or assistants in an attempt to increase efficiency and to lower the client's expenses. This can be a huge benefit to the client - providing a system for efficiently handling the case and a "point person" for the client to talk to for administrative needs.

However, other firms look at associates and assistants as an additional stream of revenue. In these firms, associates and assistants may be expected to meet their own quotas for "billable" time, generating enough revenue to cover their salaries and firm overhead expenses. The associates and assistants may handle the majority of your case, with little oversight from the attorney you thought you were hiring.

In firms with multiple staff members, how are communications and training managed? If you talk to an assistant or an associate, how will the information be communicated to the attorney handling your case and other members of the firm? You don't want to spend your time explaining the situation to one person to then have to explain it again to your attorney. How will you be billed for time spent on your case by different staff members? It is common to charge for time an associate or assistant spends on your case, but you don't want to also be charged for time spent within the firm to communicate about your case, for attorneys to give instructions on tasks or for assistants to ask questions clarifying assignments.

What is the firm's reputation?

Does the firm participate in any service projects or pro bono activities? Is the firm a "fly by night" operation or one concerned about building a business within the community? Is the firm involved with community events and organizations?

A firm that is concerned about building a solid business within the community will be involved in community events and will sponsor community organizations. A firm that is just interested in making a quick buck; or a lawyer that is in business until the next thing comes along won't take the time to build a community-oriented reputation.

Are the lawyers able to provide testimonials from previous clients? Are reviews available online on independent websites such as Avvo or Google Local? More and more our society is turning towards online reviews to evaluate and choose potential service providers and this can be a helpful way to evaluate a law firm. But at the same time, keep in mind that attorney's ethic rules can provide restrictions in how testimonials are used. It is not uncommon for a disgruntled opposing party to leave bad reviews online for the other side's lawyer. If you find a negative review online, don't be afraid to ask the attorney about it.

What is the firm's general approach to providing services?

Does the firm provide any information, resources, or handouts for free? Or does it operate on a "nothing in life is free" model? Does the firm provide any educational services? The type of information, resources, and educational services a firm makes available to the general public can provide great insight on how the firm generally approaches business. A firm that provides free resources is concerned about more than just making money.

When working with clients, does the firm look at the big picture of the client's needs? Does the firm consider how the legal case is impacting other areas of the client's life and business? Does the firm suggest ways the client can be proactive in resolving future conflict? Does the firm build relationships with clients designed to last beyond the initial matter?

All of these factors can provide insight on how a business is being managed and may predict the quality of their work, and the reasonableness of your legal fees. Before hiring an attorney take the time to learn about their business and understand how the firm operates.

Chapter 4
5 Lawyers to Watch Out For (And One More Legal Threat)

While there are thousands of lawyers out there, if you are concerned about getting quality legal service without being taken for a ride there are five types of lawyers you must be aware of:

1. The Big Fancy Lawyer

The lawyer that gives the rest of us a bad name, the Big Fancy Lawyer (BFL), is concerned about maintaining a big fancy lifestyle – the downtown office space, the luxury car, and the designer clothes. BFL views clients as dollar signs, not people, and would rather run up the fees than solve the problems of the client. The law firms owned by BFL often have large overhead expenses to keep up with. BFL will get what he or she can from the client, and as soon as the client runs out of money BFL will drop the case (preferably before having to go to trial).

Despite having paid way too much money, clients of BFL will know next to nothing about the court process, the law, or reasonable settlement options. BFL's abandoned clients will feel completely unprepared to handle the case without legal assistance, and may not have enough funds remaining to retain a new lawyer.

2. The Jack of All Trades Lawyer

The Jack of All Trades Lawyer (JoATL) can be the most difficult to spot. There are countless areas of legal practice, each with its own complex rules, procedures, and nuances specific to that area. While there are many decent lawyers with successful general practices, some lawyers who practice in multiple areas of the law become a JoATL.

A JoATL takes any type of case that walks in the door, but does not take the time to learn the specific rules and procedures for every area of practice. JoATL may know just enough about each practice area to be dangerous. You run the risk that JoATL will cost you money by not being up to date on the law relevant to your case or by missing important steps or procedures in your case.

When interviewing an attorney with several different areas of practice, take care to ask questions pertaining to the lawyer's experience with your type of case and the steps the lawyer takes to keep up with new developments. Ask the lawyer specific questions on what you can expect during your case as far as the court process, the legal documents, and other issues that may arise. Be aware of vague or evasive answers. There are many lawyers who are good general practice attorneys, and there are many lawyers who diligently learn a new practice area, but there are also many JoATLs waiting for your business.

3. The Too Much of
a Lawyer Lawyer

This lawyer enjoyed law school a little too much and still finds great enjoyment in using impressive legal terms. Instead of thinking through the situation and considering the practical implications, the Too Much of a Lawyer Lawyer (TMoaLL) focuses his or her time on coming up with every possible legal theory and strategy that could be applied – all at a cost to the client. TMoaLL has a difficult time speaking in plain English or discussing the everyday impact of the law and legal process.

This lawyer does not feel like a lawyer unless he or she is researching various legal theories and strategies. The TMoaLL may drag out the legal process, raising your costs and ultimately achieving the same result. If you are not careful, TMoaLL will substantially increase the fees you pay just to satisfy the desire to feel like a lawyer.

4. The Starving Lawyer

In today's economy, the legal job market is tough. Many big firms have laid off attorneys. Every six months a new batch of lawyers pass the bar exam and are sworn in. The market is flooded with lawyers looking for a job. Many lawyers are desperate for any type of legal work. The Starving Lawyer (SL) will try hard to get your business. While the SL has several concerns of its own, they may also be a TMoaLL or a JoATL with all of those concerns as well.

Oftentimes SL will quote you prices dramatically lower than any other lawyer. An important thing to keep in mind with SL is that the appealing low price may very well end up costing you more over time. While SL's hourly rate might be half as much as other lawyers, SL may spend three times as long on your case. Perhaps because SL has too much time on his or her hands and nothing better to do than work on your case and bill you for it, or perhaps SL's inexperience and inefficiency requires SL put more time in on your case. Ten hours at $200 an hour is $2,000. Thirty hours at $100 an hour is $3,000. Beware of the SL – a low-ball price may end up costing you.

#5. The What You Want To Hear Lawyer

This lawyer will agree with everything you say and make you believe that you will get everything you want. The What You Want to Hear Lawyer (WYWTHL) will never tell you that you might be wrong or that you are being unreasonable. Settlement is almost never discussed with a WYWTHL. The WYWTHL is not concerned about educating you on the legal process or telling you what a reasonable outcome might be. Instead, you will hear a considerable amount of "I understand," "I'm angry for you," and "I can make the other side pay for this." This lawyer will take your money, take your case to trial, and not care about the result.

Be aware of the WYWTHL. Sure, some people are initially put off when their lawyer tells them, "You are being crazy and unreasonable. You should give up that notion and start focusing on settlement." However, often those clients end up avoiding the expense of a losing fight.

#6. The Not a Lawyer Lawyer

In addition to the five lawyers to watch out for, there is one more legal threat you need to be aware of: The Not a Lawyer Lawyer (NaLL). This can be an independent paralegal, someone who has had "experience" (perhaps their own divorce or lawsuit), a company that prepares legal forms, or an organization that plays off your emotions.

NaLL cannot give you legal advice and cannot represent you in court. NaLL may sell you pro se legal forms that you can find for free at the courthouse. While NaLL may help you fill out the forms, NaLL does not have the knowledge or expertise to craft documents that will meet your goals or gain court approval. When you initially hire NaLL there may not be a full understanding of what services are or are not included.

NaLL tends to be significantly cheaper than a lawyer, but all too often people who fall victim to a NaLL find themselves spending more money on attorneys trying to correct the problems created by the NaLL. Do your pocketbook a favor – skip the NaLL and save a few hundred dollars.

Chapter 5
Don't Try This At Home!

More and more often, people are tempted to handle their cases without a lawyer. We all want to think we can do things ourselves. Thousands of forms can be found on the Internet, many for free. There are all sorts of Not a Lawyer Lawyers offering their services for a fraction of the cost of a qualified lawyer.

But just because you *could* do it without a lawyer does not mean you *should*. Think of all the other people you pay to take care of you and your family – doctors, car mechanics, plumbers, electricians, hair stylists.

If you need surgery you would not perform it yourself. You are also not thinking of paying someone who has merely seen or experienced a surgery to perform it for you.

While there are many books available explaining how to change your car's oil, fix a plumbing problem, or install an electrical outlet, most of us realize our own limitations and the value of making sure things are done right. We will gladly pay a professional to handle those tasks.

Unless you have a very simple hairstyle, a remarkable ability to handle a pair of scissors on your own head, and really don't care how you look, you will pay for a haircut without thinking twice.

Still, many people think they can be their own lawyer without suffering any consequences. It is a regular occurrence for an attorney to be contacted by potential clients who tried to handle their own legal matters and are now looking to fix the problems they created. Unfortunately, by this time there is rarely a quick fix. If these people are lucky, a lawyer might be able to correct their mistakes, but it will likely cost them more than if they had hired the lawyer to handle the original matter.

Sometimes, by going without a lawyer, you create a problem that cannot be fixed – you miss important deadlines; you enter an agreement where you failed to understand the long-term consequences; you end up with a final decree that cannot be modified. There is an old Latin saying that our legal system relies on – *ignorantia juris non excusat* – ignorance of the law does not excuse.

If you choose to proceed without a lawyer, you are acting as a lawyer. This is true even if you have paid a paralegal to prepare your divorce papers or purchased a will over the Internet. You are expected to know the same laws and procedures as any other lawyer, and you will not get a second chance to fix things just because you chose not to do it correctly the first time.

Don't let the fear of legal fees get in the way of obtaining legal advice. Spending the money now might be a tough pill to swallow, but it is likely to be well worth it in the long run.

Chapter 6
Choosing an Attorney
5 Things to Consider

Once you understand how legal fees work and which lawyers to watch out for, it is time to think about how to choose an attorney and what to expect from an attorney. While it would be possible to write an entire book on this topic, here are five things to consider when looking for an attorney:

#1. **Where to Find an Attorney**

The first step in choosing an attorney is to know where to find one. Years ago the answer was simple - look in the phonebook. But these days few use the phonebook, or advertise in it. These days, the Internet has taken the place of the Yellow Pages. Search the Internet for attorneys in your area who handle the type of cases you have. Many bar associations will also maintain a directory of local attorneys.

The best place to find an attorney can be through personal recommendations. Ask your friends and family about any attorneys they know or who they have used.

Ask attorneys you or your friends know and trust, and don't be afraid to ask for a recommendation to another attorney. For example: if you need a business attorney, but your best friend really loved her divorce attorney, call the divorce attorney, explain who you are, and ask for a referral to a business attorney.

#2. Initial Consultations

There are many misconceptions about initial consultations. Don't be fooled by the lure of a "free initial consultation." Many potential clients believe a free initial consultation is a chance to get all of their legal questions answered by an attorney for free, while many attorneys believe a free initial consultation is an opportunity to present an individualized infomercial on why the client should hire them. Because so much in the legal world is fact-specific, it is nearly impossible, and rarely advisable, for an attorney to provide definitive answers to legal questions in the environment of an initial consultation. And no potential client wants to be subjected to an individualized infomercial about the attorney.

Not all attorneys provide a free initial consultation. Some attorneys will charge their full hourly rate for an opportunity to meet and discuss your situation. Other attorneys may have a specific consultation fee. Once again, the time constraint and nature of the consultation can prevent the attorney from providing definitive answers to the client's legal questions. If the client is paying full-price for the "privilege" of meeting with the attorney there can be little incentive to hire the attorney to handle the case.

The initial consultation is designed to provide an opportunity for you and the attorney to meet each other, evaluate the situation, and determine if there is a mutual desire to work together. In an ideal world, the initial consultation would allow each side to learn about the other and form a mutually beneficial working relationship. At a minimum, an initial consultation should cover the basics of who you are, what type of case you have, what experience the lawyer has, how the lawyer charges, and what you could expect by working with the lawyer.

While the initial consultation is not the place to get legal advice, an initial consultation is a great opportunity to learn generally about your case and the law. What issues are you facing? What is the general process for cases like yours? What are reasonable outcomes?

Before scheduling an initial consultation, understand how the attorney treats them. What is the cost for an initial consultation? What can you expect from the initial consultation? Is there anything you should do beforehand to prepare for the initial consultation?

#3. Hourly Rate vs. Income

One common misconception about lawyers and legal fees is the idea that a lawyer's hourly rate has a significant impact on the lawyer's personal income. For most employees in most industries, an hourly rate multiplied by the number of hours worked equals the income received. However, that is simply not the case when it comes to lawyers.

A lawyer's "hourly rate" is their rate for billable time - time actually spent working on an hourly case. There is plenty of work that lawyers need to do that is simply not billable - administrative work, client development, education, networking, etc. Just because a lawyer is working forty or more hours a week, does not mean a lawyer is generating their hourly rate for every hour worked.

From the money a lawyer does generate, there are certain expenses that must be paid simply to stay a lawyer. This includes attorney's license, bar memberships, malpractice insurance, continuing legal education credits, and for many attorneys, payments on student loans. This is in addition to all the business expenses that come with running a firm. These expenses typically include rent, utilities, supplies, staff, and taxes. Only after all of these expenses does the lawyer actually receive an income. A lawyer charging $200 an hour may only be earning income equal to $20 an hour.

#4. The Attorney's Approach

The approach an attorney takes when handling a case can have a big impact on the direction your case takes: from the overall outcome, to your legal fees, and your satisfaction with the process. An attorney who looks at the big picture will treat the case differently from an attorney who only looks at the immediate issue. By looking at the big picture, both the attorney and the client can stay focused on important issues without getting caught up (and spending too much time, money, and emotional energy) on things that may not matter in the end.

An attorney who starts out with the end in mind and considers different settlement options will be different from an attorney who immediately starts preparing for trial. Well over 90% of all cases settle before trial, do you really want to pay for a trial you will likely never need before trying to settle the case?

An attorney who takes a complete approach, who considers all areas a client may need help with, will provide a greater level of service and guidance than an attorney who only thinks about the limited situation in front of them.

#5. Your Attorney is Human Too

In choosing and working with an attorney, it is important to keep in mind that your attorney is human too. They have their own lives and their own families to provide for. Their job is being a lawyer. While you likely only have one legal case and one attorney, your attorney has several clients and several cases to handle.

While it is important to understand how legal fees work and to choose an attorney who charges reasonably, you cannot expect an attorney to work for free, or to continue working on your case if you stop paying. Attorneys have their own bills to pay and their own families to feed. In no other field would an employee be expected to continue going to work if their boss stopped paying them, but for some reason an expectation exists that attorneys should continue working under the promise of future payment.

While you ought to expect your attorney to return emails and phone calls within a reasonable period of time, you cannot expect your attorney to immediately respond at all hours of the day. Your attorney will need to spend time working on other clients' cases and should also be spending time at home not working. While it is not uncommon for attorneys to spend time working in the evenings and weekends, most attorneys attempt to work typical business hours. If you need an attorney who is available after-hours, be sure to ask if this is possible before retaining the attorney.

Chapter 7
Seven Tips That Can Save You Thousands in Legal Fees

Everyone wants to know how they can minimize their legal fees. Some attorneys will work with you to keep your costs down and tell you how you can minimize fees. Unfortunately, not all attorneys are up front about this. Here are seven tips that can save you considerable money on legal fees:

#1. Choose the Right Attorney

This is the most important tip anyone could offer. Choosing the wrong attorney will cost you dearly. Your choice of lawyer will have a significant impact on how your case is handled and how much it costs.

While it is possible to switch attorneys in the middle of your case (it happens all of the time, for a variety of reasons, and sometimes it is necessary), doing so can cost you extra for the "catch-up time." You also run the risk of your first attorney costing so much that you no longer have funds available to retain another lawyer. Most lawyers are cautious in dealing with potential clients who have changed attorneys multiple times, and it is hard to be sympathetic to a potential client claiming financial hardship when they have already spent $20,000 on the wrong lawyer.

Before hiring a lawyer, take the time to really interview potential attorneys. Find an attorney who cares about your case and who takes the time to explain the legal process and his or her services. Look for an attorney who will have an honest and frank conversation with you about your case and his or her fees. Trust your gut and choose the attorney you feel most comfortable with, even if that attorney initially costs a little more.

#2. Understand the Fee Agreement and the Office Policies

The fee agreement (or retainer agreement) will determine how you are charged and what you are charged for. The office policies will also influence how much your case costs.

Read the fee agreement closely and ask plenty of questions. If you are billed hourly, what time are you charged for? How is time calculated (in increments of one-tenth an hour or one-quarter of an hour)? What is the minimum time increment you will be billed for? If you are entering a flat fee agreement, what is included in the fee? What happens if your case requires additional services? What costs are you billed for? If multiple people are working on your case, how are you charged? How is the work divided?

How does the office policy differ from the terms of the fee agreement? How are phone calls, voicemails, and e-mails handled? What is the policy for handling copies and mail? What payment (or retainer) is required upfront? If the initial retainer runs out, will you be expected to pay an additional retainer or pay for fees on an on-going basis? What are the policies related to billing and collections?

Some attorneys may have a short and vague fee agreement that does not completely address the fees and billing procedures you could expect. Other attorneys may have a long and complete fee agreement, but do nothing more than flip to the last page and ask you to sign. Before signing any retainer agreement, it is important to take the time to read the entire document, ask questions, and fully understand the expectations. You should understand how much you will be charged, how those charges will be calculated, and how you will be billed.

Yes, it does take time to go over the agreement page by page and ask questions. Some people are uncomfortable spending so much time analyzing the retainer contract, but it is important to fully understand the fee agreement you are entering into and understand how the attorney's office operates. If you do not take the time to understand these things up front, you may suffer sticker shock when you open your first bill and realize you were charged at least $50 for each e-mail, phone call, or letter as well as an additional $75 for postage and time spent stuffing envelopes.

If your agreement requires you to provide an additional retainer upon the depletion of your initial payment, you may unexpectedly find yourself with three days to pay $3,000 or find a new lawyer (who will also require a retainer payment). Before you hire a lawyer, make sure you understand the fee agreement.

#3. Be Prepared

Do Your Homework. Look for an attorney who will spend the initial consultation providing information on your legal issue, discussing the process, and explaining what you can expect. The initial consultation is not the time or place to answer all of your questions and solve your legal disputes; it should provide you a general road map for your case. Be aware of the "free initial consultation" that is nothing more than a personal commercial for the attorney to convince you to sign the retainer agreement. Ask questions about the law and process and try to understand what you are getting into from the beginning.

Once you hire a lawyer, make it a priority to talk to your lawyer about the important issues in your case, the court process, the lawyer's suggested strategy, and reasonable settlement expectations. Don't wait until your case is almost over and you feel lost to ask about your options. You will save money by educating yourself on the process and your options up front.

The easiest way to increase your legal fees is to pay your attorney to gather and organize the information needed for your case. Most attorneys have a client questionnaire asking for information on your situation – ask for one and fill it out completely and legibly. Ask what type of documentation your attorney will find helpful (i.e. bank statements, court documents, business records, property information) and provide your attorney with well-labeled copies. In litigation cases, it is helpful to provide your attorney with three sets of copies (one for your attorney, one for the opposing side, and one for the court). Keep a set of copies for your own file.

Providing your attorney with a giant box of unorganized documents, or failing to provide your attorney with any information at all is a surefire way to add to your legal bill.

#4. Communicate Effectively

A voicemail that just says "call me" or an email that says "let's schedule a meeting" will get you nowhere. There is nothing more frustrating than getting stuck in an endless game of telephone tag. When communicating with your attorney, whether through voicemail, email, or in person, try to be clear about what you want to communicate and the next step. Keep in mind that each phone call and email may cost you so make it count.

When scheduling a meeting or returning a phone call, specify times when you are available. If you are providing information to your attorney, be sure to specify whether you expect a response or just wish to convey the information. Leave a detailed message about what you need and utilize your attorney's staff when possible.

#5. Use the Lawyer's Time Wisely

Keep in mind that while you only have one lawyer, your lawyer has several clients. For your lawyer to be able to work efficiently on your case (as well as the other clients' cases) and to keep your legal fees reasonable, it is important to use the lawyer's time wisely.

Make sure you understand what is going on with your case, the law, legal process, and your lawyer's advice. If something is unclear, ask your lawyer to explain it to you. Don't wait until it is too late – as this can cause all sorts of expensive problems. To avoid asking the same questions over and over, take notes when talking to your lawyer. Keep a notebook to help you stay organized.

Instead of calling or e-mailing your lawyer each time you think of a question, make a list of questions to ask in one phone call or e-mail.

One of the most important ways to use your lawyer's time wisely is to keep your lawyer informed about the relevant case information, but do not spend the time using your lawyer as a therapist.

Your lawyer needs to know if your soon to be ex-spouse is using drugs and alcohol, and can answer questions about how that might impact the divorce and custody decisions. No matter how much you talk about it, your lawyer will not be able to answer why your ex started using drugs and alcohol, why it took you so long to realize it, what you could have done differently to address the problem, or if your ex will ever be clean, sober, and responsible again.

#6. Be Reasonable

Reasonable expectations lead to reasonable fees. Yet for many, all reasonableness is lost when faced with a legal battle. Sometimes your lawyer might tell you something you are not ready to hear. It is too easy to get caught up in the emotions of the case. Whenever possible, treat your legal case as a business transaction. Take a moment to step back and assess the situation. Unfortunately, many lawyers will play into a client's desire to fight, even if this approach costs thousands of dollars more.

#7. Keep in Mind the Cost of Fees

Most people will agree that it makes no sense to spend $10,000 to get $5,000 back, yet this is an everyday occurrence in the world of litigation. People tend to lose their common sense when dealing with the stress and emotions of a lawsuit. All lawyers have stories about the crazy things people do when caught up in the moment.

Know when it is time to let go. Take a step back and try to approach your case like a business transaction. A courtroom is not the proper place to address issues better suited for therapy.

Chapter 8
The Value of a Lawyer

Are you still worried about legal fees? Are you still considering representing yourself due to the fear of high legal fees? Yes, attorneys can be expensive. And choosing the wrong lawyer can leave you with a high legal bill. But going it alone can also cost you. Here are just a few examples to illustrate how important choosing the right lawyer can be.

Ann and the Crazy Charging Lawyer

Ann and Brad have been married for nearly thirty years. They have six children together; three of them are still at home. Throughout their marriage Ann has stayed home, caring for the kids. She plans to go back to school when her children are all teenagers. She has always been interested in medicine and kids – maybe she'll become a pediatric nurse or a midwife. Brad works full-time, and in his spare time operates a very small landscaping business. Combined, Brad's income from these jobs is less than $75,000 per year. Ann and Brad have lived a modest life. Although they do not have any debt, they also have very little in savings, a small 401(k) through Brad's employer, and less than $20,000 of equity in their home.

After many years spent unhappy in his relationship, Brad tells Ann he wants a divorce and he is moving out. Brad's leaving caught Ann by surprise, and she's very angry about it. This is not the way her life was supposed to go. She is also scared of what will happen now. She has been out of the workforce for over twenty-five years. Brad's income has paid the mortgage and the grocery bill. Ann does not know what to do on her own.

Brad has hired a lawyer for the divorce, and Ann knows she should too. Ann first meets with Tom, a lawyer recommended to her by a friend at church. Tom is a small firm lawyer who only handles family law cases. He charges $200 per hour. Tom talks about marital division of property, child support, and spousal maintenance. Tom sees that there are not enough assets or enough cash flow to sustain Ann's way of life. Tom tells Ann that while she will receive child support from Brad, she will not receive enough (if any) spousal maintenance to pay her bills. Tom asks Ann what she plans to do to earn money. Ann takes this question as a personal attack. Brad is the one who wants the divorce, Brad is the one changing the plans he and Ann had made, the plans they built their lives around.

Why should Ann have to a worry about finding a job now? Ann does not like what Tom has to say and does not want to work with him.

Next, Ann meets with Karen. Karen is a well-known attorney at the largest firm in their city. From their first meeting, Ann clicks with Karen. Karen understands why Ann is angry. Karen assures Ann that Brad will have to pay her enough child support and spousal maintenance so she can pay her bills and not worry about finding a job. She will be able to stick to their original plan, be home with her children for few more years, and then go back to school. She won't have to work until she is done with school, in seven or eight years. Karen seems just as irritated with Brad's decision to divorce as Ann is. Ann really likes everything Karen has to say.

At $350 per hour, Karen's rates are higher, but she has a lot of experience with divorces. Karen works closely with her assistant Shannon, whose rate is only $85 per hour. Ann chooses to hire Karen. She uses her savings account to pay the initial $3,000 retainer payment.

Karen gets started working on Ann's case. After receiving the initial divorce pleadings, Karen serves out formal discovery requests. She also schedules a temporary relief motion hearing. Karen tells Ann this is necessary to protect her. Before the first hearing Brad and his lawyer make a settlement offer. The terms of the settlement offer look a lot like what Tom had said to expect. But Karen assures Ann she can get more. She can make Brad pay.

The first invoice Ann receives from Karen's office looks a lot like this:

Staff	Rate	Description	Total
Shannon	$85.00	Set up client file. .5	$42.50
Karen	$350.00	Review client file. Instructions to Shannon to schedule temporary hearing and draft standard discovery so I can modify it. 1.5	$525.00
Shannon	$85.00	Schedule temporary hearing. Memo to Karen re: date. .4	$34.00
Shannon	$85.00	Work on standard discovery. Ask Karen questions. .7	$59.50

Karen	$350.00	Questions from Shannon on discovery requests. .5	$175.00
Karen	$350.00	Do calculations for child support and maintenance. .8	$280.00
Karen	$350.00	Last time did not calculate child support correctly. Recalculate. 1.9	$665.00
Karen	$350.00	Receive court assignment. .1	$35.00
		Postage	$15.00

Ann is so overwhelmed by the whole process she does not question the invoices she receives from Karen. In fact, she barely even looks at them.

After three months, Ann has run out of money with Karen and needs to make another payment. The next month Ann is able to put $1,000 on a credit card as payment for her legal fees. The following month she comes up with $500 in cash to pay Karen. That is still not enough. Ann asks her parents, her sister, and her best friend for help. Ann borrows money from everyone she can and is able to pay another $2,000 over the next three months. These payments still do not keep up with Ann's ever-increasing lawyer bill. When Ann is unable to pay anymore to Karen, Karen withdraws from the case. At this point Ann owes Karen over $15,000 in legal fees.

Ann has spent everything she has and has borrowed from everyone willing to loan her money to try and pay Karen. Ann can no longer afford to hire another attorney and must complete the divorce on her own. Because Karen has been guaranteeing Ann will get enough spousal maintenance to pay all of her bills, Ann is unwilling to consider any other settlement offers. The case ultimately goes to trial, two years after the divorce started.

Meanwhile, Karen tries to collect from Ann the outstanding legal fees owed to her. Karen charges Ann an additional $2,250 in legal fees (after having withdrawn from the case) for the work done to recover these fees. Karen is able to place an attorney's lien on Ann's home in the amount of $18,000, depleting any equity Ann had in it.

When all is said and done, Ann incurred over $24,000 in legal fees. Ann spent all of her savings. Because she borrowed money and used a credit card to pay some of her legal bill, she now has debt. There is no longer any equity in the house. Ann spent the past two years waiting for the large settlement Karen said would come. But the judge did not award her enough spousal maintenance and did not order Brad to pay for her legal fees. Ann spent two years and $24,000 waiting for something that is not going to happen. Ann now needs to figure out how to find a job to support herself and pay her debts.

The Uncontested Divorce

Ian and Jamie have been married for five years when they decide to divorce. Their daughter, Kelly, is three years old. Ian and Jamie get along well enough and want to have an amicable divorce for the sake of their daughter. They don't see a reason to spend money on lawyers when they have an agreement about everything. Jamie gets the divorce papers from the court's website and together they start filling them out.

Ian and Jamie have agreed to equally split everything: cars, bank accounts, and retirement accounts. Jamie wants sole physical custody of their daughter, but has agreed to the parenting time schedule Ian requested - which is almost half the time. Kelly is with her dad every Tuesday and Thursday overnights, and every other weekend from Friday evening to Sunday night. Ian and Jamie have also agreed to disregard the guideline child support calculations and have set the child support payment at $200 per month.

Ian and Jamie submit their pro se papers to the court, and within a couple months their divorce is finalized. Everything seems to be going smoothly. Ian buys himself a new house and Jamie starts dating a new man. About a year after the divorce things start to fall apart.

The relationship between Ian and Jamie has deteriorated since the divorce. Jamie gets remarried and moves with Kelly, nearly an hour away. With Kelly's new home and new daycare an hour south of Ian's home, and Ian's job thirty minutes north, his Tuesday and Thursday overnights become logistically impossible. When Kelly starts school, Ian's parenting time becomes limited to every other weekend.

Ian has lost considerable time with his daughter due to his ex-wife's move and the reality of school, work, and traffic. Jamie is unwilling to agree to give Ian additional weekends or time during the summer to make up for the lost time. The final straw comes when Jamie asks for more child support - guidelines support of $800 per month. Ian does not know how he will keep up with his own bills.

Ian meets with family law lawyer Lisa to ask what he can do to keep the original agreements from the divorce decree - $200 per month in child support and nearly half time with his daughter. Lisa reviews the divorce decree Jamie and Ian had drafted and delivers the bad news to Ian. The document he had filled out and signed provided him no protection against these changes. While he could ask a court for more than every other weekend, he is unlikely to get as much time as he had before and the child support will likely increase by $600 per month.

The Importance of Modification

Greg and Hanna are the parents of three kids, Iris (5), Jackson (10), and Katie (15). When Greg and Hanna decide to divorce they proceed pro se using free forms available off the Internet. The divorce decree states Greg is to pay $900 per month in child support until the youngest child turns 18 or graduates from high school

Greg begins to dutifully pay the $900 per month in child support. When Katie turns 18 and graduates from high school, he wonders if his child support will be reduced. He even asks his child support worker about it, but all she says is he should speak to an attorney. Greg does not have the money for an attorney, so he just continues paying his $900 per month. He finally decides to speak to an attorney as Jackson's high school graduation approaches.

After speaking to the lawyer, Greg learns that a court would easily lower his child support due to the change in minor children. All he would have to do is bring a motion to modify child support. Had Greg asked for a decrease after Katie's graduation, his child support would have been lowered to $700 per month. Had he lowered his child support at that time, Greg would have saved $12,000 in child support over the five years since Katie's graduation. Unfortunately, Greg cannot go back in time to ask for this adjustment.

Greg does hire the lawyer to modify his child support based on Jackson's pending graduation. The court calculates child support based on only one remaining child and orders Greg to pay $450 per month instead of $900. Greg spent $2,500 on his lawyer to get the child support modification. Because of the modification, Greg's child support has decreased by $5,400 a year for the next five years.

A DIY Estate Plan

Nora and Paul were in their fifties when they met and fell in love. They were married after a whirlwind romance of only three months. It was a second marriage for both of them. Nora's first husband had left her a widow with two children. Paul had divorced his first wife, the mother of his two children, after thirty years of marriage. Nora and Paul's marriage came as a shock to all of their (now adult) children. While Nora's children could see their mother's happiness and tried to accept Paul, Paul's children had no interest in welcoming Nora, or her children, into their lives.

After getting married, Nora and Paul talked about their estate plans. Since they each had children and adequate assets of their own, they felt it was best to have the children inherit instead of leaving anything to each other. Paul bought a couple of DIY Will forms from the bookstore and they each completed one, leaving all of their property to their own children.

Nora and Paul had twelve years of a happy marriage before Paul started suffering from dementia. Taking care of Paul and keeping him safe became Nora's full-time job.

Nora's health started deteriorating as well until the day she died of a heart attack.

While Nora's children started the process of planning their mother's funeral and handling her estate, Paul's children took over as his caregivers. Paul's dementia was so advanced he was unaware of the loss he suffered. The relationship between Nora and Paul's children had never improved during this time.

When Nora's children attempted to probate their mother's will it was challenged by Paul's children as guardians for their father. The DIY will was found to be invalid by the court - the proper procedures for leaving out a spouse had not been followed. The majority of Nora's estate was left to Paul. Had Paul been aware of the situation, he would have happily transferred these assets to Nora's children. But Paul's mind had long ago left him and his children were now in control of his affairs.

Nora's children received only a small share of their mother's (and what was their father's) estate. When Paul died a year later, his children received all of Paul's estate, including most of the assets that had belonged to Nora.

Remember...

Hiring the wrong lawyer, or failing to hire any lawyer, can cost you thousands, wreak emotional havoc, and have long-term unintended consequences.

Hiring the right lawyer can make things easier for you and your family, for years to come. Money spent on the right lawyer will be well worth the cost.

Conclusion

I understand legal fees can be overwhelming. And we've all heard the horror stories about how expensive lawyers can be. I have seen firsthand how these horror stories can get in the way of people seeking the legal help they need and the problems that arise when people attempt to find "cheaper" alternatives. I know that the value of hiring the right lawyer can save you and your family money and headaches in the long run.

I hope you have found this book helpful in understanding legal fees and how lawyers work. I hope you feel empowered to ask the right questions and make the right decisions when it comes to choosing and working with a lawyer. I hope that after reading this book a fear of legal fees is no longer a barrier in seeking the legal advice you need.

If you have found this book helpful, please pass it along to any friends or family that could benefit from it - or send them to www.LewisKLaw.com/legal-fees-book to request their own copy.

Appendix A
Questions to Ask Before Retaining a Lawyer

Choosing the right lawyer is the most important step you can take. Before retaining the services of a lawyer make sure that lawyer is the right fit for you and your case. Here are some questions to ask before hiring a lawyer:

- What is the lawyer's experience?

- What type of cases does the lawyer routinely handle?

- What counties does the lawyer typically appear in?

- Does the lawyer have experience with your type of case? With your county?

- What does the lawyer do to keep up to date on legal developments?

- What resources does the lawyer use for education, training, and keeping up to date?

- Who will be working on your case? What will their roles be? How will you be charged for this work?

- If you have questions about your case, who should you contact?

- What is the best way to contact your attorney? When can you anticipate a response?

- When is your attorney generally available for phone calls and meetings? When does your attorney respond to emails?

- What fees can you expect? What type of fee? How is the fee calculated?

- What costs can you expect in addition to legal fees?

- If you have questions about your bill or the legal fees you have incurred, who should you ask?

- What is the lawyer's general approach to cases?

- What approach will the lawyer take with your case?

- What can you do to help control your legal costs?

- What information will the lawyer need from you?

- What is the most efficient way for you to provide this information?

Appendix B
Retainer Agreement Checklist

Before signing any retainer agreement, make sure all your questions have been answered and all of the terms have been explained to you. Here are some important terms that should be covered by the retainer agreement:

- Does the agreement lay out the specific matter the law firm is being retained for?

- Does the agreement describe any services that the law firm is not providing? Does it place limits on the lawyer's representation?

- Do you know which lawyers, assistants, and other staff at the firm will be working on your case?

- What type of legal fees does the agreement cover? Contingent? Flat fee? Hourly?

- How much is the fee or what is the basis for the fee?

- If a flat fee, what is included in that fee?

- If an hourly arrangement, how is time calculated?

- How will payment be made? How much do you need to pay upfront?

- How you will be invoiced?

- What happens if you fail to make payment?

- What happens if you run out of money?

- Does the attorney require an additional retainer payment prior to trial?

- What additional costs and expenses can you expect?

- How are costs and expenses handled? Will these fees come out of your retainer payment? Will you need to pay them separately? Will they be paid to the law firm or to someone else?

- How does the attorney/client relationship end? When can your attorney withdraw from your case? If you want to fire your attorney, how do you do that?

If there is anything in the retainer agreement you do not understand, be sure to have it explained to you before signing. Remember, a retainer agreement is a legally binding contract!

Appendix C
A Client's File

By maintaining your own file for your case you will have an organized place for all information on your matter. If you have any questions about your case, you can first check your own file before contacting your attorney – saving you money in the process. Your own file should be divided into seven sections:

1. **Representation** – This section should contain a copy of your signed retainer agreement and all invoices you receive. If you receive any letters or other documents from your attorney concerning their representation of you or the attorney/client relationship, keep those here.

2. **Tasks, Deadlines, and To-Dos** - Use this section to keep a running list of tasks, deadlines, calendar dates, and to-do lists. A simple glance at the page will tell you what's coming up in your case and what you need to do.

3. **Court documents or final signed documents** – Use this section to maintain all court documents or final signed documents on your case. These are often the most important papers in your case.

4. **Notes and Communication** – Use this section to keep a log of communication between you and your attorney. Take notes on the questions you ask and the answers you receive. If your attorney has provided any informational brochures or resources, those should also be kept here. When you have a question about your case, refer to this section to see if your attorney has already provided the answer.

5. **Information** – Keep a copy of your completed questionnaire here. Also use this section to keep copies of all documents provided to your lawyer or discovery documents that are exchanged.

6. **Correspondence** – In some cases you will be inundated with paperwork, including letters to and from your attorney, the opposing counsel, the court, evaluators, mediators, and other professionals. Use this section of your file to keep track of all of these letters.

7. **Drafts and Other Papers** - Use this section for drafts of documents and other papers from your case that don't fit under any other section.

About The Author

Jennifer R. Lewis Kannegieter is a mother, a Minnesota estate planning and family law attorney, founding lawyer at Lewis Kannegieter Law, Ltd., and *Your Minnesota Family Lawyer*.

Jennifer has seen how the fear of legal fees and lawyers can cause additional stress and conflict during stressful times. She wrote *The Insider's Guide to Legal Fees: What You NEED To Know Before Hiring an Attorney* to combat this fear.

Jennifer R. Lewis Kannegieter

Jennifer provides stability and security to families while taking a three-pronged approach to her practice based on the importance of family, education, and common sense. She maintains an extensive directory of resources on her firm's website and is active in community education efforts. Jennifer has authored many articles on estate planning, family law, and working with lawyers, and is the author of the book *Why Every Adult Must Have A Health Care Directive*.

Jennifer resides in Monticello, Minnesota with her family where she is an active member of the community and a member of the Monticello Women of Today. For more information visit her website at www.LewisKLaw.com.